Maine Coon Cats

by Meredith Dash

Visit us at www.abdopublishing.com

Published by Abdo Kids, a division of ABDO, P.O. Box 398166, Minneapolis, Minnesota 55439.

Printed in the United States of America, North Mankato, Minnesota.

032014

092014

 PRINTED ON RECYCLED PAPER

Photo Credits: Glow Images, Shutterstock, Thinkstock

Production Contributors: Teddy Borth, Jennie Forsberg, Grace Hansen

Design Contributors: Dorothy Toth, Renée LaViolette, Laura Rask

Library of Congress Control Number: 2013952418

Cataloging-in-Publication Data

Dash, Meredith.

 Maine coon cats / Meredith Dash.

  p. cm. -- (Cats)

ISBN 978-1-62970-009-0 (lib. bdg.)

Includes bibliographical references and index.

1. Maine coon cats--Juvenile literature.   I. Title.

636.8--dc23

                    2013952418

Table of Contents

Maine Coon Cats

Maine coons are often called "**gentle** giants." They are larger than most cat **breeds**. They are kind and gentle.

Maine coons have thick, beautiful fur. Their fur keeps them warm in cold weather.

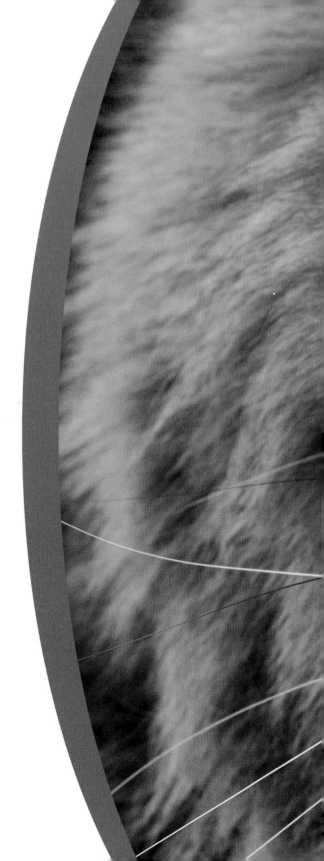

Maine coons come in
many different colors.

Maine coons **rarely** meow.

They often make a **chirping**

noise instead.

Personality

Maine coons are **energetic**.
They like to play fetch and
catch mice!

13

Maine coons like the water.

They are good swimmers.

15

Maine coons are very smart.

It is easy to teach them

new tricks.

Family Friendly

Maine coons get along with everyone, including dogs! They make great family pets.

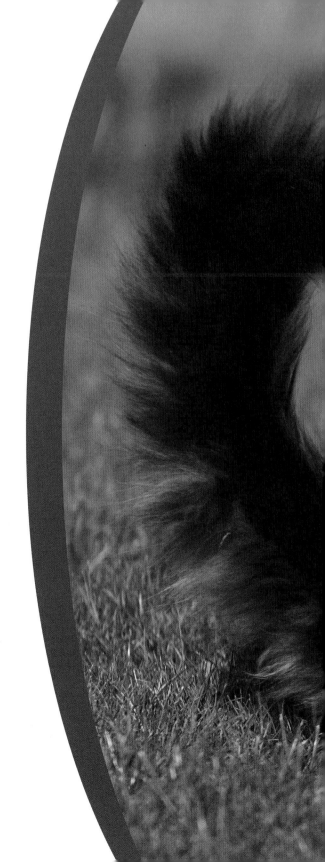

Maine coons love to spend time with their human families.

More Facts

- The Maine coon is the official cat **breed** of Maine. Maine is the only state to have a state cat.

- A Maine coon's coat gets thicker in the winter to keep it warm.

- It takes about 4 to 5 years for the Maine coon to become fully grown.

Glossary

breed – a group of animals sharing the same looks and features.

chirp – short, sharp, high-pitched sounds.

energetic – active and full of energy.

gentle – calm and sweet.

rarely – not usually.

Index

abdokids.com

Use this code to log on to abdokids.com and access crafts, games, videos and more!

Abdo Kids Code:
CMK0090